Business & Goals Workbook For Independent Artists

Create your step-by-step roadmap for a successful transition from hobbyist to an artist in business

Part of the Artist Business Success Academy

Copyright © 2020 Laura Thorne. All rights reserved.

This is an original work of Laura Thorne Consulting and copying any parts of it for commercial use is not allowed.

Business & Goals Workbook For Independent Artists

Table of Contents

Preface 2

1. Business Foundation: Who are you? 3

2. Customer Profiles: Who do you journey with? 7

3. Visioning Exercise: Where are you going? 11

4. Goals to Tactics: How will you get there? 14

5. Staying the Course: Maintain Focus 22

6. Taking the Next Steps 23

Welcome!
Artist Business and Goals Workbook

Artists operate in a world somewhere between hobby and full-blown business. Artist business owners often start out as sole proprietors and later venture into small production or retail. Almost always, the goal is to be self-sufficient enough and generate enough income to quit the day job.

This workbook is for fine artists, serious crafters, authors, painters, photographers, sculptors, ceramicists, designers, etc.

If you are looking to make a living from selling the art that you create, this workbook is for you. It is intended to walk you through just enough proven business concepts to get your business framework together and a basic strategy (we call Roadmap) to help you make real advances towards your goals without getting lost in a sea of information.

Note that this workbook focuses on the business side of marketing and selling art, and it is work. To run a successful business you need dedication, persistence, consistency, and above all, you must stay positive and excited about your art. Most artists just love making art and thus avoid "businessing" because it is not the fun part. We encourage you to add creativity into the business side so you can enjoy doing it too.

The first part of the workbook is all about strengthening your foundation so you can move forward with focus to make a bigger impact. The second part will help you to get clarity around what you want to accomplish with your art over time. The third part will help you create real actionable goals. The fourth part will help ensure that you are creating robust and actionable goals. Finally, the last two pages of this workbook will help you to put your Roadmap into action.

I'd say good luck to you, but I prefer to say, get out there and make your own luck!

- Laura

1a. Artist Business Foundation

Defining Your Artist Business: Structure & Operations

This is the snapshot of your business, a clear picture of who you are, what you do, why you do it, and what makes you and your art unique. The following are elements of your business that should be well-defined and put together with purpose and intent in order to make the most impact.

Business Name:
Your expertise (product/craft/service):
Who plays a role in the success of your business:

List your sales avenues: *Examples: craft shows, website, commissions, galleries*	**What's going well or not well in these avenues?**
List all the ways you communicate with your customers: *Examples: website, blog, Facebook, Instagram, Etsy*	**How can you improve?**

1b. Artist Business Foundation

Define Your Mission

Having a clear Mission helps you to make better and faster decisions that will have a bigger impact towards your goals. These are often not easy, especially for artists. You will refine them as you continue to think about them and become more self-aware about how they affect your business decisions and outcomes. Use this worksheet to frame and understand your unique Mission.

Your Why

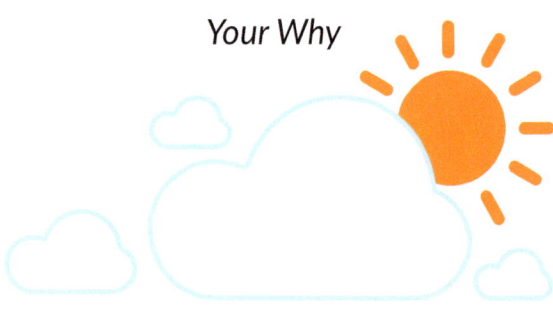

Problems You Solve

Your Mission

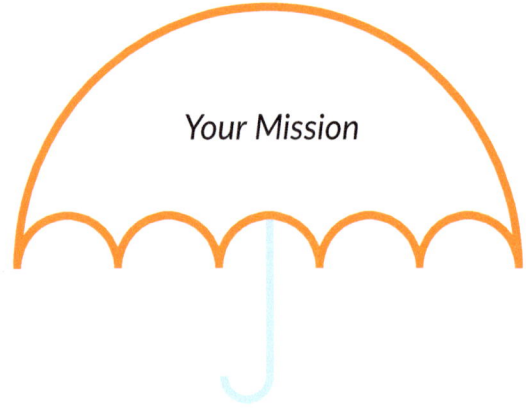

Solutions You Provide

See examples at artistbusinessworkbook.com

Step 1: Define your why: what motivates you to create your art?

Step 2: What problems do you solve for your customers? If this is difficult to answer, try doing the Customer Profiles first.

Step 3: What is your mission? Craft a simple statement of what you do and for who.

Step 4: What solutions do you provide to your customers with your art and mission?

1c. Artist Business Foundation

Build Your Values-Based Brand

A strong brand means recognition, authenticity, familiarity, and enhanced connection with your customers. It also establishes your uniqueness and will make the marketing and design of your business elements more effective and efficient, meaning less work!

Values are an important part of a strong brand. They allow you to have stronger messages and work that resonates more deeply with your best customers. Some artists have a hard time aligning their personal and brand values. Should you decide that they are different be sure to the decision is made with purpose and intent.

List 3 - 5 of your most important Values:

There are millions of ways Values can materialize in your brand. Here are just a few examples (more at artistbusinessworkbook.com):

- A love of animals might translate into a pet portrait service
- Promoting mental health might translate into a line of products that share stories
- Fighting for racial justice might translate into a bold tagline

Go back and look at your existing work: what Values do you see?

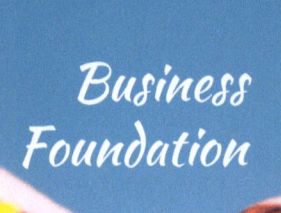

1c. Build Your Values-Based Brand, Continued

Describe the colors, fonts, and personality of your messaging

What is your brand's overall style or feel? For example, are you professional, bold tones or are you fresh, pastels, and a soothing feel?

Colors:

Fonts:

Personality:

Brand incorporation & consistency checklist

Is your brand reflected in the following? If not, brainstorm how you can edit them to include elements of your brand listed above.

- ☐ Business Card
- ☐ Social Media
- ☐ Marketing
- ☐ Your art and services
- ☐ Website
- ☐ Emails
- ☐ Invoices
- ☐ Messaging

What ideas do you have to improve your artist marketing messages and brand elements?

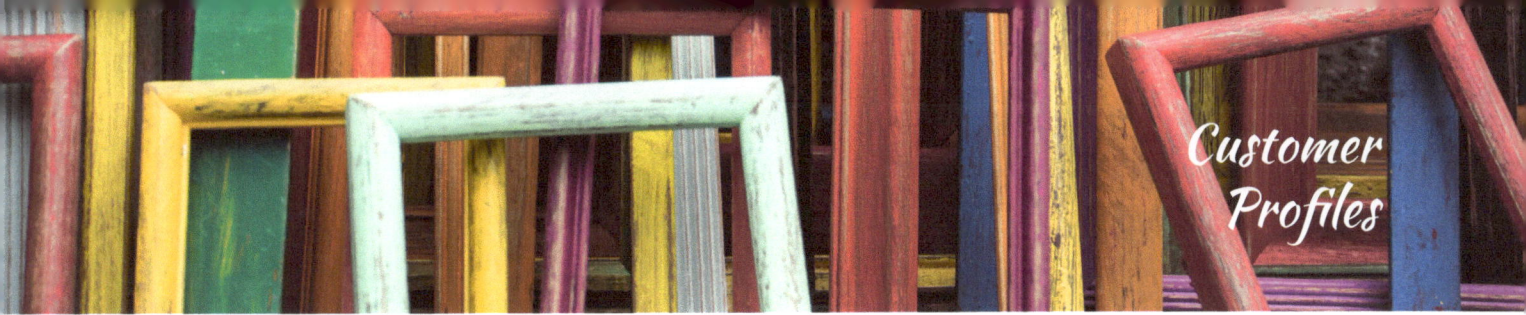

2. Customer Profiles

Understanding the Requirements of Your Artist Business

Once you have a solid understanding of what your artist business looks like, you need to have a clear understanding of who your customers are to deliver those services effectively. This activity is challenging but worth it!

This page shows the customer profile exercise template with examples and questions to stimulate your responses.

3 blank sheets are provided. This is best done with data from actual customer data and surveys. However, most artists do not have this, so use what you know and start making efforts to collect this type of information.

Customer Profile Name:
Examples: actual person's name or something like "holiday shoppers," "high-end art show," "craft fair visitor," "single mom," "gift-giver," etc.

Demographics:
Examples: Name, income, city/neighborhood, profession, marital status, kids, where they went to school, pets, political views, hobbies, where did they attended school, etc.

A day in the life:
Examples: Where do they go? Where do they shop? Where do they eat? What do they eat? What do they read? What news do they watch? Social Media platforms?

What motivates them to buy your art?
Examples: Connection with the story, right price, etc.

Goals & fears:
Can your art help them meet a goal or avoid a fear?

- Personal   · Family   · Business   · Health

What do they Value?
Examples: Healthy living, higher ed, eco, organic, handmade, custom, unique, trendy, recycling, history, family, friends, animal rights, other causes they support, etc.

What prevents them from buying?
Examples: Can't see how it applies to them, can't think of someone to buy for, etc.

Key findings:

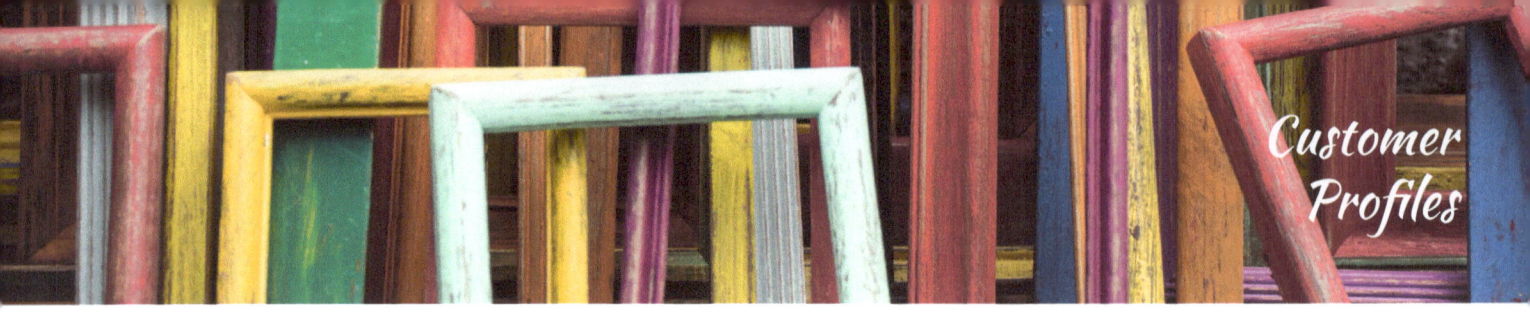

Customer Profile 1

Understanding the requirements of your artist business

Customer Profile Name:

Demographics:

Goals & fears:

A day in the life:

What do they Value?

What motivates them to buy your art?

What prevents them from buying your art?

Key findings:

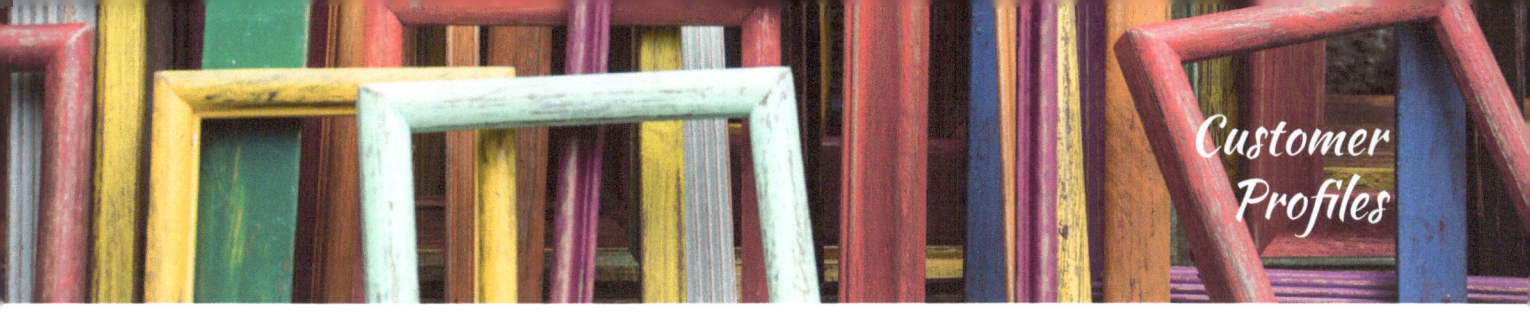

Customer Profile 2

Understanding the requirements of your artist business

Customer Profile Name:

Demographics:

Goals & fears:

A day in the life:

What do they Value?

What motivates them to buy your art?

What prevents them from buying your art?

Key findings:

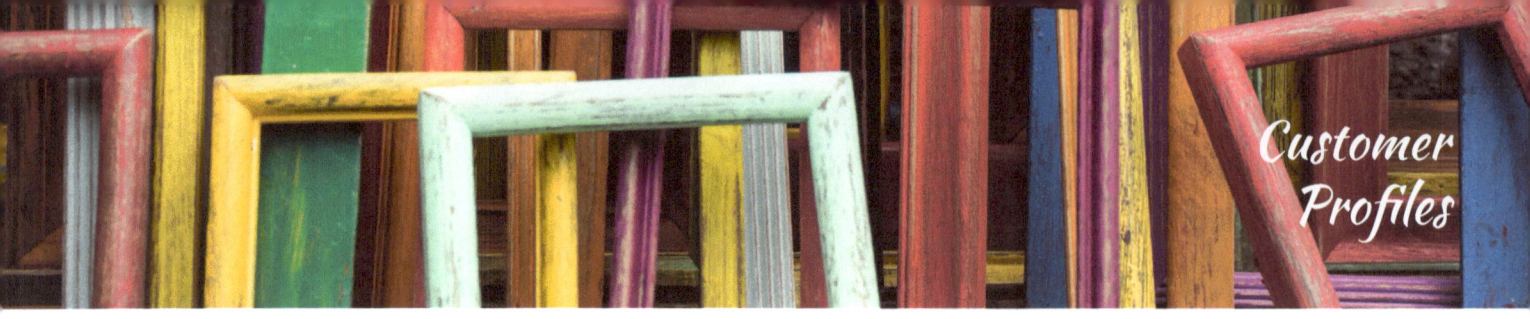

Customer Profile 3

Understanding the requirements of your artist business

Customer Profile Name:

Demographics:

Goals & fears:

A day in the life:

What do they Value?

What motivates them to buy your art?

What prevents them from buying your art?

Key findings:

3. Visioning Exercise

Creating the Link Between Now and Goals for the Future

You now know who you are and more about the customers that are with you on your journey: now we'll look at where you're going. On the next 3 pages, you are asked to visualize your artist business journey. The more vividly you can picture what you want, the more clearly you can set the path. We've provided space for you to draw what you see and feel. We suggest that you revisit this exercise routinely.

Step 1 — Picture it: me and my art now

What am I doing with my art now?

What is going well?

What am I struggling with?

Draw or sketch it:

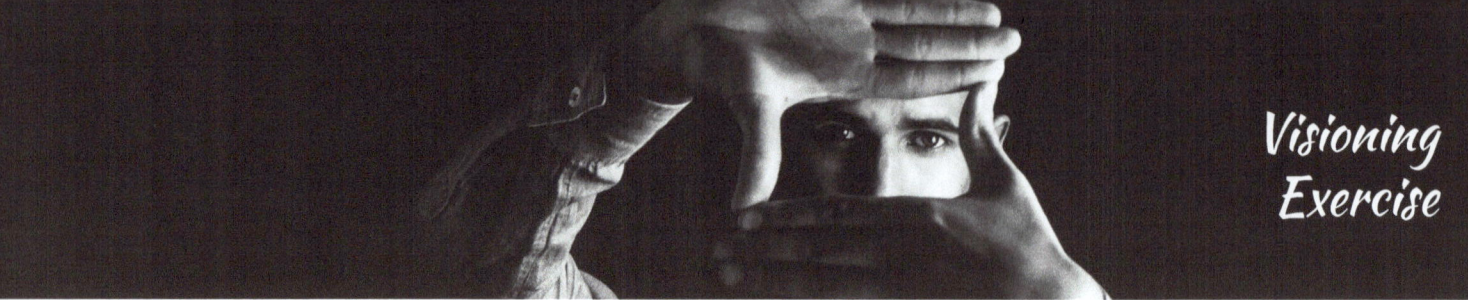

Visioning Exercise, continued

In the second step of the visioning exercises, think forward 5 years, 10 years, or longer. Write and draw what your business and life look and feel like.

Step 2 — Picture it: me and my art in the future

What does the future of my business look like?

What are people saying about my art?

Who is talking about my art?

What am I doing? (Painting? Lecturing? Selling? Teaching?)

What does the future with my art feel like?

What am I not doing anymore? What did I change or give up to get here?

Draw or sketch it:

Visioning Exercise, continued

Here, in step 3, is where your Roadmap starts to take shape. Review your responses to the previous two questions. What's missing between where you are now and the vision you drew for yourself? Answer these questions as best you can so that you can start planning to address them sooner rather than later.

Step 3 — Picture it: What's missing to make your vision reality?

What am I missing to get there?

What do I need to learn, borrow, or buy?

Who do I need to meet?

Draw or sketch it:

4a. Goals to Tactics: Definitions

Align, Integrate, and Prioritize!

One area in which artists have a disadvantage, compared with people trained to think strategically and business-like, is the ability to clearly articulate and craft actionable goals. Actionable goals are aligned to your Mission and are prioritized so that you work on the ones that will get the best results now. Not everything has to be done at once, and some actions we think we should take really shouldn't be done at all.

This section will teach you how to craft actionable goals, show you how to brainstorm business ideas, and get them ready for the last section where you will choose what to work on. You'll start on this page defining goals and on the next pages creating a balanced set of goals to move your business forward!

TACTICS: the tasks, activities, and projects you need to do to achieve your GOALS

SMART GOALS: Specific | Measurable | Achievable | Relevant | Time-bound

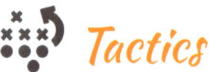 Tactics

- Take a sewing class
- Make a Facebook post every day
- Sign up for the summer vendor show

 Goals

- Learn to sew
- Increase Facebook likes
- Make more sales

 Broad Goals

- Learn to sew
- Increase Facebook likes
- Attend more art shows

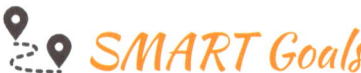 SMART Goals

- Learn to sew within 6 months
- Register for and attend 3 vendor shows this year
- Update and publish new website by end of June

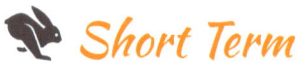 Short Term

Near future goal. Sometimes a goal will be met and can be placed. Other times there can be a long term goal attached.

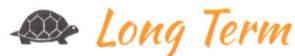 Long Term

Set a 3, 5, or even further out goal to help act as your guidepost, which will help you make better short term decisions.

4a. Goals to Tactics: Definitions, continued

Now that you have a better understanding of how to craft clear goals. You'll use the next 4 pages to brainstorm goals for each of the 4 areas of business that should be addressed to achieve steady growth, reduce risk, and keep you on track towards your vision while accomplishing your mission! Exciting, right?

The Four Key Measurable Goal Areas to achieve BALANCE:

Financial:
- Funds in/funds out, profits, payments, bills.
- Consider goals for key sales avenues or a specific customer type.

Communications/Marketing:
- Consider a goal for your key social marketing platforms, newsletter, or ad campaigns

Improvement (development and training):
- You must always be improving to stay on top.
- Consider goals related to training, learning new skills, and getting feedback.

Production/Operations:
- Purposefully considering operational goals helps ensure that you balance your ability to sell with your ability to produce.

Gather, Sort & Prioritize Ideas

Next you'll use these 4 areas to brainstorm ideas for all the various actions you could be taking to achieve your goals. You'll format them as best you can into SMART Goals. Then, you'll sort all the tactic ideas that you come up with into categories that will help you figure out what to be working on next. Finally, you'll choose just a few top priorities to get started on. This is how you get focused on the right things to include on your Roadmap.

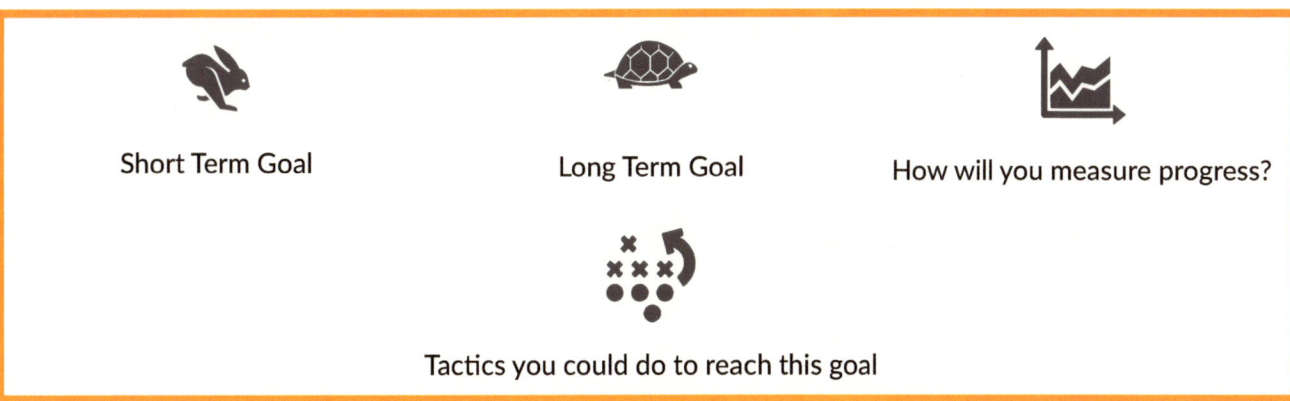

4b. Goal Brainstorming: Align, Integrate & Prioritize!

1. Write 3 - 5 SMART goals (short-term months - a year & long-term 1-3 years)
   Specific | Measurable | Achievable | Relevant | Time-bound
2. Write how you could measure them. *Not everything will have a number you can easily track.*
3. List all possible tactics you might take to achieve that goal

Financial Goals

Long Term	Short Term	How can you measure progress?	Potential Tactics
Example: Increase profit by 75% by 2021 (be Specific and Realistic. It's OK if you don't reach the goal. You'll be able to evaluate your progress and brainstorm why you're not meeting the goal.)	· Improve Branding within 1 month · Get more Instagram followers	· Monthly revenue · Number of sales · Number of profitable events	· Redesign Website · New business cards · Hire help on Fiverr · Find some Insta partners

★ Congrats, now you have a list of great ideas that are directly tied to your long and short term goals! Beware, it is counterproductive to try to work on all of them at once. Prioritize the top 1 - 3 that you will have the most immediate impact for you to work on in the next quarter (or you may determine your own time cycle) and mark them with a star or numbers. On page 20, you'll combine your priority tactics and sort them into buckets to help further prioritize your next steps.

Not sure what to put a star next to? Choose ones that come up more than once, ones that you are the most excited about, or ones that have to be done prior to several others.

4b. Goal Brainstorming: Align, Integrate & Prioritize!

1. Write 3 - 5 SMART goals (short-term months - a year & long-term 1-3 years)
   Specific | Measurable | Achievable | Relevant | Time-bound
2. Write how you could measure them. *Not everything will have a number you can easily track.*
3. List all possible tactics you might take to achieve that goal

Communications/Marketing Goals

Long Term	Short Term	How can you measure progress?	Potential Tactics
Example: Be a famous artist in my field in 10 years (don't hold back!)	Be interviewed on the top podcast in my field in 18 months	· Annual revenue · Number of exposure events	· Exhibit a solo show · Network with influential people · Seek out high end galleries · Learn more about agents

★ Congrats, now you have a list of great ideas that are directly tied to your long and short term goals! Beware, it is counterproductive to try to work on all of them at once. Prioritize the top 1 - 3 that you will have the most immediate impact for you to work on in the next quarter (or you may determine your own time cycle) and mark them with a star or numbers. On page 20, you'll combine your priority tactics and sort them into buckets to help further prioritize your next steps.

Not sure what to put a star next to? Choose ones that come up more than once, ones that you are the most excited about, or ones that have to be done prior to several others.

4b. Goal Brainstorming: Align, Integrate & Prioritize!

1. Write 3 - 5 SMART goals (short-term months - a year & long-term 1-3 years)
   Specific | Measurable | Achievable | Relevant | Time-bound
2. Write how you could measure them. *Not everything will have a number you can easily track.*
3. List all possible tactics you might take to achieve that goal

Improvement Goals

Long Term	Short Term	How can you measure progress?	Potential Tactics
Example: Be the role model in my area of expertise.	· Learn to do video presentations and demonstrations · Publish my videos	· Number of videos produced · Feedback on videos · Number of subscribers	· Research what others are doing · Take a class · Daily practice · Create my own YouTube channel

★ Congrats, now you have a list of great ideas that are directly tied to your long and short term goals! Beware, it is counterproductive to try to work on all of them at once. Prioritize the top 1 - 3 that you will have the most immediate impact for you to work on in the next quarter (or you may determine your own time cycle) and mark them with a star or numbers. On page 20, you'll combine your priority tactics and sort them into buckets to help further prioritize your next steps.

Not sure what to put a star next to? Choose ones that come up more than once, ones that you are the most excited about, or ones that have to be done prior to several others.

4b. Goal Brainstorming: Align, Integrate & Prioritize!

1. Write 3 - 5 SMART goals (short-term months - a year & long-term 1-3 years)
   Specific | Measurable | Achievable | Relevant | Time-bound
2. Write how you could measure them. *Not everything will have a number you can easily track.*
3. List all possible tactics you might take to achieve that goal

Production/Operations Goals

Long Term	Short Term	How can you measure progress?	Potential Tactics
Example: Generate ___% of my income from online courses in my online store	Expand my offerings to include an online store and course within 18 months.	· Number of modules completed · Online course sales	· Research online store options · Start outline for course · Research similar courses · Set up starter online store

★ Congrats, now you have a list of great ideas that are directly tied to your long and short term goals! Beware, it is counterproductive to try to work on all of them at once. Prioritize the top 1 - 3 that you will have the most immediate impact for you to work on in the next quarter (or you may determine your own time cycle) and mark them with a star or numbers. On page 20, you'll combine your priority tactics and sort them into buckets to help further prioritize your next steps.

Not sure what to put a star next to? Choose ones that come up more than once, ones that you are the most excited about, or ones that have to be done prior to several others.

4c. Goals to Tactics: Refine Your Priorities

Collect all the tactics you generated in the last exercise then sort them into the following groups.

- **To-Do List:** If it is simple and you can do it now: add to your to-do list
- **Roadmap:** It can be done soon or broken into smaller actions and will make a big difference
- **Parking Lot:** Something you need to do, but it will be too hard or expensive to do now: add it to the tactics in the Parking Lot and evaluate it again in the future
- **Ditch or Delegate:** The tactic does not align with your mission or you can delegate it

To Do List

Place tactics that you can implement in the next 24 to 48 hours here. You can also add tactics that are easy to complete that you can fit into small time blocks between larger tasks.

-
-
-
-

Roadmap

Place tactics that you can implement relatively easy or break down into steps to get started on now. These will become your Roadmap projects for the next time cycle.

-
-
-
-

Parking Lot

Place tactics that will have to wait here. These are ones that you don't have the resources for or they are too big or the timing isn't right. *Note: you can make a smaller starting tactic on the Roadmap.*

-
-
-
-

Ditch/Delegate

The fastest way to complete a task is to not do it at all. If there are any potential tactics that could be done by someone else, automated, or eliminated, place them here.

-
-
-
-

Access templates at artistbusinessworkbook.com

4d. Goals to Tactics: Complete your Roadmap

At this point, you have brainstormed a balanced set of goals and sorted them into timeframes for action. Here, you'll outline the Roadmap tactics on which you'll focus your efforts for the next 4 to 6 months, or until you revisit these exercises.

List the Roadmap tactics you chose from the above exercises and list them in order of which you want to complete first and break them down into smaller steps if needed. Find more examples at artistbusinessworkbook.com.

Roadmap & Action Plan

Tactic	Steps	Completion Date	Resources Needed	Budget	Obstacles
Example: Set up starter online store	1. Research YouTube & ask for recommendations	8 days	Internet time, email/call friends with stores	$0	
	2. Choose & register site on ecommerce platform	14 days	Funds and time	$30/month	How to choose a platform
	3. Design storefront	14 days	Branding details, funds, computer time	$0	Not sure what it should look like
	4. Add inventory	5 days	Images, computer time	$0	Need tech help
1.					
2.					
3.					

5. Staying the Course: Maintain Focus

For Long-Term Success, Consistency and Persistence Are Key!

These are the suggested steps to make up your art as a business Roadmap. You should adjust or customize these steps and frequencies to meet your needs. Historically, annual cycles were common; however, in this day and age of fast-paced technology and social media updates, a flexible and more ongoing method is more effective.

Add to calendar	Activity	Frequency	Next Due Date
☐	**Social media review** Are your social media and marketing efforts working?	Monthly	
☐	**Review progress on your goals (the things you are measuring).** Are you meeting your goals? If not, look into why not. If so, keep going!	Quarterly	
☐	**Review your Artist Business Foundation (section 1)** Update as needed	Every 6 months	
☐	**Priority tactics: check progress** If you completed them, select a new one.	Every 6 months	
☐	**Check for changes/risks** New/closed galleries, new/stopped events, new online store, new social media, new product, new hot topics, etc.	Every 6 months	
☐	**Priority tactics: check alignment** Are my tactics still in line with my Mission and goals?	Annually	
☐	**Review your comparisons.** Take a minute to look at who else is creating art in your space. Is anyone else doing something new and fun? Are they doing better or worse than you?	Annually	
☐	**Other key dates** Holidays, event dates, subscription renewals, vendor dues, membership dues, and reminders		

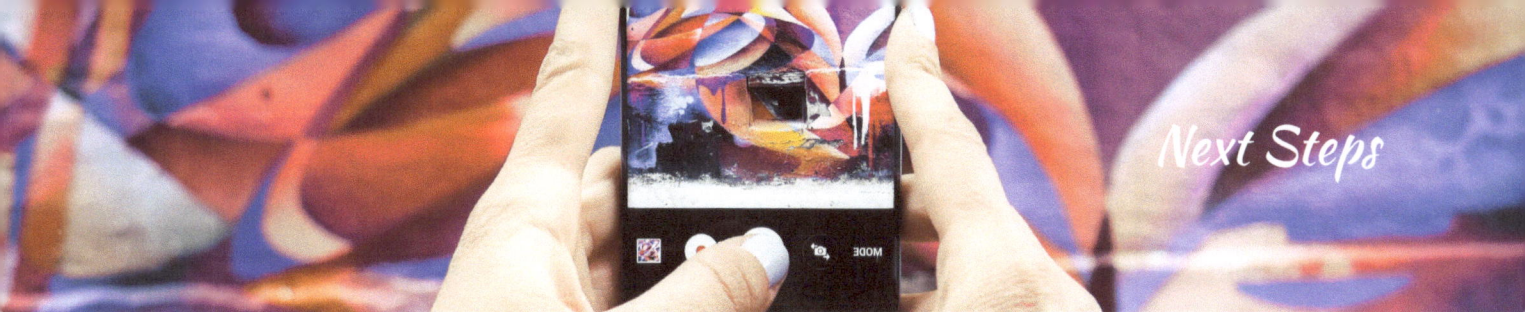

6. Next Steps

Put Your Priorities Into Motion!

In the next 24 hours, I will do the following: *See to-do list from section 4c*

In the next 72 hours, I will do the following:

How will you hold yourself accountable?

List a few comparables: Who can you learn from?

Final Note

This workbook is a brainstorming get-you-started-on-strategy exercise. Many other business practices are not covered and by no means is there any legal advice contained here. Feel free to use this workbook personally, anyway that is best for you and the performance of your artist business. Templates for the exercises and additional resources can be found at artistbusinessworkbook.com. This is an original work of Laura Thorne Consulting and copying any parts of it for commercial use is not allowed.

Celebrate small wins and stay gold!

Laura Thorne Consulting

Syracuse, NY | laurathorneconsulting.com/arts | 813-444-2622

Notes

Notes

Notes